THEN & NOW

FAIRPORT AND PERINTON

Opposite: Civic pride and family values have been the hallmarks of the village of Fairport and town of Perinton since the 1850s. In the 21st century, the town of Perinton has twice been named by *Money* magazine as one of the top 100 communities in the United States to live and raise a family. Here the Fairport Fire Department is marching down Church Street in a parade during the 13th annual fireman's convention held in Fairport in 1908. The volunteer fireman holding the flag is believed to be Charlie Hull. (Perinton Historical Society.)

THEN & NOW

FAIRPORT AND PERINTON

William Keeler and Keith Boas
for the Perinton Historical Society

*This book is dedicated to those men and women in our community
who have made their voices heard and stood up
in support of historic preservation.*

Copyright © 2009 by William Keeler and Keith Boas for the Perinton
Historical Society
ISBN 978-0-7385-6234-6

Library of Congress Control Number: 2008933720

Published by Arcadia Publishing
Charleston SC, Chicago IL, Portsmouth NH, San Francisco CA

Printed in the United States of America

For all general information contact Arcadia Publishing at:
Telephone 843-853-2070
Fax 843-853-0044
E-mail sales@arcadiapublishing.com
For customer service and orders:
Toll-Free 1-888-313-2665

Visit us on the Internet at www.arcadiapublishing.com

On the front cover: The trains are speeding down the New York Central Railroad tracks at a crossing on North Main Street. At one time, there were six railroad tracks and two railroad companies whose tracks converged in the village of Fairport. The building in the background is the Osburn house, built in 1870, razed in the 1930s, and then replaced with a service station. The building now houses a coffee shop. (Perinton Historical Society.)

On the back cover: Fairport citizens assembled on North Main Street to watch the Certo fire of 1921, which is occurring down John Street to the right. Firemen are connecting hoses to fire hydrants on Main Street and running them down the street to fight the fire. (Perinton Historical Society.)

CONTENTS

ACKNOWLEDGMENTS

Thanks go to Jean Keplinger, Perinton town historian, for her work in looking over the manuscript for errors in historical facts and allowing the author access to the town's extensive archives and photograph collection; the Perinton Historical Society Board of Trustees for allowing the authors to organize the publication of the society's third book with Arcadia Publishing; Katie Comeau, advocacy coordinator for the Landmark Society of Western New York, for her review of the manuscript and advise on historic preservation and architectural terms; and finally, Keith Boas, the photographer whose professional excellence and intimate knowledge of the community and its terrain made this book possible.

We would like to thank the following individuals and organizations for generously allowing us to use their pictures for this publication: Perinton Historian's Office (historic images on pages 23, 26, 32, 52, 53, 68, 69, 75, 76, 82, 83, 86, 87, 88, 94), Imogene Blum (historic image on page 90), Karl Jost (historic image on page 17), and Keith Boas for all of the modern images. All other historic photographs not listed above are the property of the Perinton Historical Society.

INTRODUCTION

The town of Perinton and village of Fairport are like many suburban communities throughout New York State, and they have seen similar changes over the years.

In the late 19th and early 20th centuries, there was a great deal of growth in industry that led to housing developments and businesses that provided services to support the increased population. Over time, these same businesses and houses expanded and modernized, changing the look of small towns and villages from when they were originally founded. Buildings and construction styles from one era coexist with those from other time periods. Projects from the state and the federal government sometimes radically changed the landscape. The vestiges of these projects and other changes can be seen in the built environment and in the community's attempt to incorporate these buildings into its streetscapes over the years through rehabilitation, reuse, or replacement by more modern structures. Each village and town is a conglomeration of buildings of different styles and time periods.

Even with these similarities, the Town of Perinton, incorporated in 1813, and the Village of Fairport, chartered in 1866, have handled these and other changes in unique ways over their almost 150 years of existence.

The Erie Canal, built by the State of New York and opened in 1825, transformed this rural community of several hundred souls, as the canal opened up new farmlands and markets for crops grown in the area. Warehouses were built to store produce for shipment on the canal, and hotels and stores were created to handle the people traveling along it. The first hotel built in Fairport is still standing, covered up by years of expansion and renovation so that the building is now three times as large and the original section is completely hidden from view.

Along with increased trade from the canal came industry, which thrived in Fairport until shortly after World War II. Using the canal and later the railroads to receive raw materials and ship finished goods to New York City and cities to the west, the community thrived. Industries such as Douglas Packing Company, makers of Certo brand fruit pectin; Cobb Preserving, packers of canned fruits and vegetables; American and Sanitary Can Companies, makers of the first seamless cans; and the DeLand Chemical Works, makers of the baking product saleratus, all built large and impressive factories. After these industries went bankrupt or left the area, their large buildings became homes for smaller businesses and shops.

Housing for the new workers and mansions built by newly rich owners of the factories can still be seen today on village streets. There are neighborhoods from the 1850s still sporting the familiar Greek Revival–style homes popular at the time. The house now known as the Green Lantern Inn was built by Henry DeLand, the largest employer in town, in a classic Second Empire style designed by John Rochester Thomas, who was appointed as architect for New York State in 1874. Henry DeLand was the half brother of Daniel DeLand, who founded the DeLand Chemical Works in 1855.

The rebuilding of the Erie Canal by the State of New York from 1903 to 1918 did not add houses or buildings to the landscape but did raze several early buildings that had hugged the edges of the canal for many years. The Main Street lift bridge in the heart of the village replaced a fixed steel bridge when the canal was widened from 70 to 120 feet. Buildings were destroyed or moved, such as the Hardick building, which was moved just around the corner to West Avenue.

The centralization of the Fairport School District in 1955 made many small one-room schoolhouses obsolete. There were 11 one-room schoolhouses, many of which have been rehabilitated into homes and businesses.

With the introduction of the automobile in the early part of the 20th century, it seemed that the large oil companies had a master plan to buy up every major street corner in America and put gasoline stations on them. In Fairport along Main Street where State Routes 31F and 250 run together, there have been 11 gasoline stations built in the last century. Of these, only two remain. Most of the rest of the buildings have been rehabilitated, reused, and melded into the community.

The 1970s brought the shopping mall onto the American scene. A federal program of urban renewal was offered to many villages as a response to this changing business climate. One large block in the South Main Street business district was destroyed along with a large section of property along the barge canal. The buildings were replaced by a park, parking lots, and pseudohistorical buildings to make it look like a period canal town.

In the late 20th and early 21st centuries, there has been a trend by drugstore chains to purchase multiple properties in small towns and villages, raze the existing structures, and build large one-story drugstores. The congregation of a large 19th century church on the corner of Main and Church Streets was approached by a developer willing to purchase the church and raze it for commercial use. The outcome for this property has not yet been decided.

Change does not happen without dissent. As early as 1903, a series of editorials were written denouncing the enlargement of the canal through the village. Citizens felt that too many buildings located beside the canal would be destroyed and that enlarging the canal might attract surly characters that would work on the state project. Several village officials lost their political lives with their stand on urban renewal. The newly elected mayor in 1977 succeeded in saving the 1912 lift bridge but saw the destruction of over 40 buildings in the South Main Street and West Avenue business districts. In 2007, in response to an offer by a developer to purchase a church and demolish it for commercial development, the officials of Fairport passed a historic preservation law to protect the ambiance of the village.

Looking at the pictures in the book, one may gasp in horror at what has been lost or agree with the choice to raze a run-down building and replace it with a more modern and efficient structure. Similar changes have been made in other communities. Change is inevitable but it can be directed. Scale, size, and harmony are important and should be major factors in decisions for change.

Historic preservation was a choice for the people in Perinton who supported a historic preservation law in 1987. Now Fairport has enacted its own preservation law in 2007. Both laws were passed to keep a balance between uncontrolled building projects and a small-town feeling and ambiance that attract people to this place. In the end, it is all about choices. The one thing to remember is that the building usually outlasts the business, and it is up to the citizens of each generation to decide how to incorporate these structures into the community or replace them with something that keeps the feel of the community intact.

CHAPTER 1

HOMES AND HAUNTS

Where people live and hang out are important in their lives. Distinctive houses or special places only known by local people add to one's sense of place. Fairport Road was once a two-lane dirt road crossing Irondequoit Creek near an old local mineral spring in the woods. Today it is a four-lane road entering the village of Fairport.

Henry DeLand, owner of the DeLand Chemical Company, had this Second Empire–style house built in 1876 from a set of plans drawn up for his half brother Daniel DeLand, who suffered an untimely death at the age of 49. In the 1930s, Pure Oil Company leased the front lawn of the property for a gasoline station. The cottage-style building was designed by C. A. Petersen in 1927. This is one of only a handful of service stations in this style still standing today.

The pergolas and garden were built for Frank Holmes and his wife Victoria, who bought the Henry DeLand house in 1923. Holmes, who made his money exporting lead and zinc, brought in hundreds of European plants and roses for the garden and hired an English gardener to tend them. After the house became a restaurant, the gardens were removed and replaced with an expansion of the dining facilities and a parking lot.

This typical Greek Revival–style house stands in the village of Fairport at 78–80 West Avenue. The house was once occupied by prosperous businessman G. L. Seeley while his brick mansion was being built across the street at 83 West Avenue. When this house was first built in the 1850s, the village had only dirt roads. Wooden sidewalks were installed to keep much of the dirt out of the house and keep women's skirts out of the mud in the spring.

One of the oldest houses in the hamlet of Egypt is the Ramsdell-Ranney house, built by Thomas Ramsdell in 1815 and inhabited by the Ranney family from 1862 to 2000. In 2001, the inside was gutted in preparation for an ice-cream shop as part of Egypt Plaza. The plans never materialized, and the building was bought by a neighboring landscape company that uses the building as an office to sell brick and stone pavers.

Known today as the Potter Community Center, this house was originally a large Italianate house bought by Alfred Potter, son of Henry Potter, vice president of Western Union. With the inheritance left to him from his father, Alfred added two large gabled dormers, a wrap-around porch, and a porte cochere. His son Frederick left the house and five acres of land to the Village of Fairport in 1943. The interior was remodeled in 1944 by local architect Henry Martin.

RESIDENCE of A.B. POTTER,
FAIRPORT, N.Y.

Isaac Hastings traveled west on the Erie Canal and moved into this house in Bushnell's Basin in 1834. He lived here until 1855 or 1856 when he and his wife moved to New York City. The house burned down in 1920. The site is now part of the Bushnell's Basin Preservation District, the first designated district in the town of Perinton.

Dr. Walter Payne was a veterinarian who ran a small practice on West Avenue. He is seen posing with his wife Elizabeth and son George in front of their home at 39 West Avenue around 1910. The Paynes were in their 30s and George was two years old. The house was taken down in 1977. The site is now the back side of the Fairport Village Landing Mall.

HOMES AND HAUNTS

Around 1913, Payne and his family moved to 92 South Main Street. Comparing this picture with the one on page 18, Payne still has his right hand on his hip, Elizabeth is still sitting on the front porch, and George, sitting on his tricycle, is now five years old. The house was replaced by Hupp Motors in 1920 and by the DeLand Center in 1963, which serves as a meeting hall for the First Baptist Church next door.

Monroe County acquired the former Rand's Powder Mill in the early 1930s, created a park, and renamed the property Powder Mills Park. The many hills supported trees that provided fuel for the making of dynamite and protected the residents from explosions. Roland Stevens, a Dartmouth College ski jumper, proposed that a ski jump be built on the property, and in 1935, the largest one in western New York was built. The ski jump, called Powderhorn, was dismantled in the early 1980s.

For years, this house was known as the Mulliner house. It was owned by Ellen Mulliner, who, after her husband died in 1870, ran a boardinghouse for single female teachers who taught just down the street at the Fairport Union School. In the 1920s, the house was bought and converted to a gasoline station. Later the house was torn down by Socony Oil Company, and a modern gasoline station was constructed on the site.

The pierced vergeboards of this Gothic Revival house were the most distinguishing feature of Rev. F. M. Straight's home, built about 1852. This was once the home of Edward and later Frank Bown, sons of George Bown. Bown and Sons made carriages just across South Main Street until 1887. That year, the buildings burned, and the business was relocated closer to the canal in the middle of the South Main Street block.

This magnificent house was built by spice manufacturer William Newman in 1856. Newman had another grand house built on West Church Street and sold this one to Yale Parce in 1872. The house was on the grounds of the Parce and Solly Nursery for many years. The large porches were removed, and the walls were covered with vinyl siding. The building is now occupied by a realty company and several small businesses.

The house on the right was once the home of Levi DeLand, owner of the DeLand Chemical Company. Built in 1888, the house sat on 200 acres of fruit trees and nut groves. In 1904, the house and property were sold to the Baptist Home. The building to the left was dedicated in 1914. The main house was razed in the winter of 1971 and replaced with this new building in the summer of 1973.

BAPTIST HOME, FAIRPORT, N.Y.

BUSINESSES
AND INDUSTRY

As the population of the area increased, more industries moved into the area, spawning more shops and businesses that catered to the new residents. Nelson's Store, built in 1895 in the hamlet of Egypt, served the community for several generations. In 2004, the store was destroyed by the New York State Department of Transportation so that it could relocate the intersection of Loud and Mason Roads.

One of the buildings slated for demolition when the Erie Canal was rebuilt was the Hardick and Fellows Book and Jewelry Store, built in 1874. The building is one of three sections of a block that was bought by Frederick Schummer. This section was moved around the corner from South Main Street onto West Avenue in 1912. Later the front of the building was faced with brick and was a showroom for Taberrah Motors, which sold Pontiac automobiles.

The Filkins Block at 45 South Main Street was once the home of Filkins Meat Market. In the 1920s, the ground floor was occupied by Fairport Motors, which sold Buicks and had gasoline pumps on the sidewalk facing South Main Street. The building was bought by Fairport Savings and Permanent Loan in 1938. At that time, the third floor was removed, and Slocum Insurance Agency occupied the second floor.

The Osburn House, with the distinctive mansard roof, was built in 1870. The hotel was the scene of a bank robbery by two men in 1896. Fred Woods, one of the robbers, was caught in Rochester and sent to prison. After getting out of jail, Woods robbed the hotel again in 1908 and got away with $20 and a shot of whiskey. The hotel was razed in 1938 and replaced with a gasoline station, which is now a coffee shop.

Osburn House and N. Y. C. Fght. Office, Fairport, N. Y.

On the corner of North Main Street and John Street, now called Liftbridge Lane, was the Queen Anne–style Cottage Hotel built around 1886. A third floor was added in 1889 along with a 60-foot-long annex. There was a disastrous fire in 1968 that resulted in the building being torn down that same year.

Kettler's Garage was one of two gasoline stations on the corner of Baird and Fairport Roads, the other being the Underpass Garage. Early gasoline stations used existing buildings or houses and installed gasoline pumps and outdoor hydraulic lifts to repair automobiles. Later stations were built with indoor lifts so repairs could be made in all types of weather. The site is now occupied by a local frozen custard shop and insurance agency.

The Italian Renaissance–style Temple Theater was opened in 1927 at 87 South Main Street. There were three businesses in the building, a tailor shop on the north side, a sweet shop on the south side, and the theater in the middle. This brick structure, with cut-stone face, was built with fire safety in mind and had five fire exits. In 1958, the building was sold to the Fairport Masonic Lodge for $30,000. The lodge added a brick facing and gabled entrance.

Looking at North Main Street from the Main Street bridge, some of the very first buildings in Fairport are visible. The first hotel in town, known as the Cyrus Mallett Inn, is the first building on the left. Later it was combined with the building next door, and a third floor was added. It is known today as the Millstone block. The three-story building in the middle is the Boyland Mill, which was moved to John Street in 1915 to make way for the Rochester, Syracuse and Eastern Electric Railroad station. Today this building is a small sewing supply store.

Lucas and Purcell's Saloon at 53 North Main Street is decorated with patriotic trim and a welcome sign for old home week and the fireman's convention of 1908. This was one of several bars located next to the train tracks of the New York Central Railroad and the West Shore Railroad. This area was known in the early 20th century as whiskey flats. The building is still a local bar.

In the 19th and much of the 20th century, many American homes were heated by coal. The Loomis Coal yards, one of three at the time in Fairport, was located on High Street just north of the New York Central Railroad tracks. Loomis had a railroad spur behind the building to unload product. The company also sold vegetables from its office. Today there is a parking lot for shops next door to the former warehouse and Catholic church, built in 1856.

Known as the Chase Block, Stillwell's Grocery Store supplied food to people who lived north of the canal. Fairport's first public telephone was installed in this building, which housed McBride's Grocer in 1942 and Messerino's Food Store in 1947. The building was destroyed by fire in 1977. The site is now occupied by an animal hospital.

After World War II, a unique style of building entered the American scene. Quonset huts were built extensively in the Pacific for airplane hangers and barracks during the war. Their design shed water easily, and they were simple to build. The Quonset Inn was a restaurant and night club on Fairport Road just outside the village of Fairport. For many years, it was Fairport Hardware, later became a church, and is now a garden shop.

Church Motors on the corner of South Main Street and Pleasant Avenue incorporated the Quonset hut style into its showroom. Built in 1953, the building was designed by the Rochester architectural firm of Martin, McGraw and Winard. Church Motors had 6,000 square feet of floor space and sold Dodge and Plymouth automobiles. A realty company bought the building in 1987 and added offices onto the front of the building.

The Cobb Preserving Company was located at the eastern end of the village on the south side of the Erie Canal. Founded in 1877, the company canned local fruits and vegetables. The buildings were built very close to the canal, and defective cans of product were often dumped in the water. The company stayed in business until around 1908. In 1952, the buildings were purchased by Crosman Arms, makers of air rifles. Today the remaining buildings have small shops.

The Cox Shoe factory was built in 1884. This was the site of the famous shoe worker's strike of 1890. Workers from this factory, upset over unfair wages and layoffs, caused a nationwide strike. In 1904, the factory was bought by the Sanitary Can Company, which was acquired by American Can in 1908. Before American Can moved out in 1984, 21 connected buildings were added to the original structure. The original building now houses a used business furniture outlet.

Food processing has always been important in Perinton and Fairport. The Egypt Canning Company was located in the hamlet of Egypt on State Route 31. The large barn in the foreground held finished canned produce, and its location right on the street made a perfect billboard to advertise its products. The barn has been removed, and the factory building is now used as a warehouse.

The DeLand Chemical Works was the first large industry in Fairport. The original buildings pictured here were located on three acres on the Erie Canal. The company made saleratus (pearl ash used in baking) and baking soda. Buildings on the site have been destroyed and rebuilt several times, housing such varied businesses as a vinegar works, pectin factory, and a box warehouse. The site now has a gazebo and parking lot overlooking a docking area on the Erie Canal.

The DeLand factory burned down in a devastating fire on February 4, 1893. The fire is believed to have started in the building on the corner of John Street (now known as Liftbridge Lane) and North Main Street caused by a spark from a fire at the Schummers block several hundred feet away in the business district across the canal that was extinguished by the fire department the night before.

This foundation from the old DeLand Chemical Works is one of the oldest surviving exposed foundations in the village. This stonework survived the DeLand fire of 1893, the Certo fires of 1916 and 1921, and box factory fires of 1983 and 1985. In front of the foundation in the historic image are, from left to right, Will Sproul, bookkeeper; Wayland DeLand, engineer; and Harry Pritchard, salesman. From left to right in the contemporary image are Peter McDonough, Fairport mayor from 1971 to 1982; Fritz May, current mayor of Fairport; and Matson Ewell, former Fairport Museum director.

The DeLand family rebuilt the factory after the fire but shortly after went out of business. The New York State Fruit Company bought the building in 1906. Robert Douglas invented Certo brand fruit pectin in 1913 and founded Douglas Packing to manufacture the product in these buildings. General Foods operated the factory until 1946. This complex of buildings, which has small shops and offices, is now known as the Box Factory after its last manufacturing use by H. P. Neun Paper Box Company.

New buildings and storage facilities were added to the former DeLand Chemical Works property when the New York State Fruit Company took over the site. The storage and settling tanks were added for the processing of vinegar. They burned in the fire of 1921. Today there is a small gazebo, a parking lot, and docks for pleasure craft on the Erie Canal.

George B. Hart bought out the Salter Brothers Nursery in 1913. Hart's Nursery was located on Moseley Road on 36 acres just south of the village of Fairport. It specialized in roses and gardenias and raised over three million roses in 26 greenhouses. Hart's Woods Apartments were built in 1972 on 22 acres. Fourteen acres of maple and beech forest from this nursery were saved and listed in the National Natural Landmarks registry.

BUSINESSES AND INDUSTRY

Churches, Public Buildings, and Schools

Religious, public, and school buildings have always been important symbols in the community. The First Baptist Church, on the corner of Church and Main Streets, is the lone survivor of buildings that were converted to gasoline stations. Mobil, Texaco, and Gulf oil companies built or converted buildings into stations on three corners, and Tydol had pumps installed one building down from the church.

47

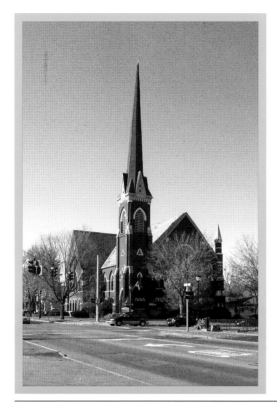

The original Baptist church was built in 1834. It was moved in 1876 to make way for the larger brick church designed by John Rochester Thomas. Considered one of the most prolific architects in the late 19th century, Thomas is credited with designing a number of public buildings in the New York City area and several churches as far south as Virginia, several of which are on the National Register of Historic Places. The sanctuary is in the shape of a cross and the church spire rises 184 feet.

The Episcopal church was built on the foundation of a previous church on the site. Rev. William Davis razed the church and began construction of this craftsman-style church. He was his own builder and architect but was helped by members of the congregation. Many of the materials from the old church were used to build this church in 1908. By 1968, the parishioners moved to a larger church, and the Fairport Fire Department built a station on the site.

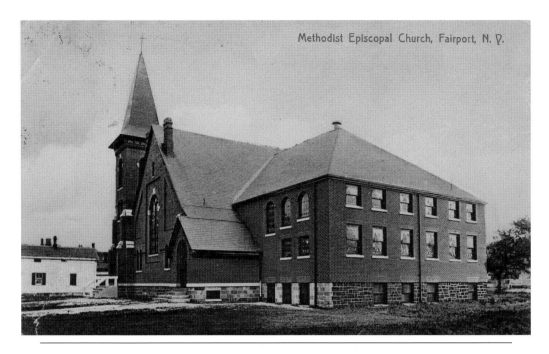

Methodist Episcopal Church, Fairport, N. Y.

The original Fairport United Methodist Church on West Church Street was built in 1879 at the cost of $15,000. Starting in 1904, the entire church was replaced with an addition designed by architects Fay and Dryer. This was followed by additions in 1953, 1964, and 1994. A fire in the 1970s caused some major renovations. In 1991, the front entry was changed to its present location.

CHURCHES, PUBLIC BUILDINGS, AND SCHOOLS

As industries like the DeLand Chemical Works and the Cox Shoe factory moved into the village, so did the Irish Catholics who worked in the factories. The Church of the Assumption was built in 1882 on East Avenue. This replaced a former warehouse on High Street where services were held. The 1882 church was torn down and a new church built in 1983, which can be seen through the trees in the center of the picture. The church bells were saved and installed in the new church.

Church of The Assumption, Fairport, N. Y.

The Midvale School on Baird Road was built in the 1880s. Once a one-room schoolhouse, the left wing addition was designed by the architectural firm of Dryer and Dryer in 1926. When the Fairport School District was centralized, this building was abandoned and proposals were made to make it into the Perinton Town Hall. The town hall eventually was built on Turk Hill Road, and this building became a restaurant and later an office building.

CHURCHES, PUBLIC BUILDINGS, AND SCHOOLS

This Italianate-style home was built as a schoolhouse in 1854. Originally it was one story, but as more funds became available, the second story was added. Henry DeLand bought the building in 1873 and converted it to a boardinghouse for teachers who worked at the Fairport Classical Union School down the street. It became the Fairport Gospel Center in 1951 and was destroyed by fire in 1970.

The Perinton Town Hall was built in 1905 and was the first public building to house all the official town records. The building was designed by the Syracuse architectural firm of Kirkland and Hallenbeck. It served as the town hall until 1931 when it was sold to the Village of Fairport for $1. The original cupola was replaced with a clock tower in 1978.

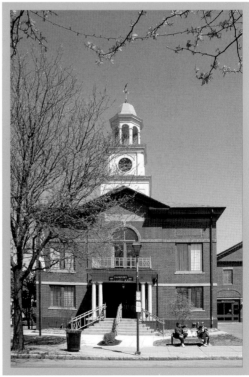

The house once owned by Frances Schummer was bought by the Fairport School District and made into a public library in the 1930s. In 1935, the house was torn down and replaced by a new brick library building designed by local architect Henry Martin. The building was a Works Progress Administration project with the community paying $40,000 for the building materials and the federal government providing the labor. In 1979, the library moved, and the building was converted to the Fairport Historical Museum. The building is the first to be selected as a local Fairport landmark in 2008.

The Fairport Classical Union School was built in 1872 and was the first high school in the town of Perinton. When the new high school was built in 1924 at the back of the property, this building became a grammar school. In 1971, it was replaced by a school administration building called the Streppa building. A proposal to remodel the outside of this building to look like the former school was defeated by voters in 2007.

CHURCHES, PUBLIC BUILDINGS, AND SCHOOLS

The Frederick Schummer house was acquired by the Fairport School District in 1916. The building was remodeled into classrooms and had grammar school classes until 1924. The art deco–style West Avenue high school was designed by Rochester architect O. W. Dryer in 1923 and opened in 1924. The school was closed in 1983, and the building was converted into condominiums several years later.

NORTH SIDE SCHOOL, FAIRPORT, N.Y.

The Northside School, built in 1886, served schoolchildren north of the canal and railroad tracks. In 1920, the tower was removed and an extension built. The building was bought by Crosman Arms in 1960 and made into a community center. The Perinton Town Recreation Department and Perinton Historical Society occupied the building in the 1960s and 1970s. The building was remodeled into senior living apartments in 2002.

CHAPTER 4

REBUILDING THE ERIE CANAL

The Erie Canal was not just enlarged from 1903 to 1918 but was totally rebuilt. The new, improved canal bypassed the three largest cities in upstate New York, entered lakes and streams, and reduced the length of the canal by 10 miles. The result was a larger, more efficient canal, and it was given a new name, the New York State Barge Canal.

Contract 63 was won by H. S. Kerbaugh of Philadelphia in 1910. The company was responsible for widening the canal and rebuilding its structures for all of Perinton from the Wayne County line to Main Street in Pittsford. This was the eighth-largest contract awarded for canal construction, coming in at $2,349,697. The canal was drained from January to May to allow for major excavations and replacements of structures such as the Main Street bridge in Fairport.

The construction season of 1912 stopped just short of the Main Street bridge and the Main Street business district. The winter of 1913–1914 saw the razing of the Hawkins Block, the two gabled buildings on the left, and the removal of the steel span bridge.

The old fixed steel bridge was removed in sections beginning in January 1914. Because of the buildings lining the street, the approach to it remained the same, and a lift bridge was designed for this site so that it could attain the minimum height of 15½ feet, as required along the whole length of the canal. The challenge for engineers was that they had to design the bridge with a 4-percent grade and 32-degree skew.

The Main Street lift bridge was designed by architect F. P. Williams and is a triangular truss style with an arched top chord. The steel for the new lift bridge was delivered in January 1914. It took three months to assemble the 139-foot-long bridge and another three months to complete the counterweight and lay the bridge floor with wood. The floor was later replaced with steel grating.

There were two steam shovels in operation in the canal prism in the village of Fairport in 1913. The canal was enlarged to 123 feet across and 12 feet deep. The soil was moved by train to spoil areas along the canal. The waste weir on the right is near Liftbridge Lane. This waste weir acts as a relief valve on the canal. When the water rises too high, excess water overflows into a ditch that flows into nearby Thomas Creek.

The Rochester, Syracuse and Eastern Electric Railroad followed the canal towpath for about a mile through the village of Fairport. This wooden fence was built to keep the trolleys from scaring the mules and horses as they pulled the barges. The trolley went out of business in 1935 and the fence was removed. Today there is a public boat launch and rental in the area. The tower on the left is a former railroad switching tower that serves as the boat rental office.

Although steam shovels were used to remove large amounts of soil, manual labor was still needed to put on the finishing touches. The men are waiting for a small dynamite charge to go off so that they can remove the excess shale and place stone blocks along the walls. The two large beams are cranes that were used to move the large blocks in place. They were designed to move from place to place and set up easily.

Some dredging near bridges was done during the summer but most of the excavating near the Parker Street bridge was done in the winter by hand. Some of the soil was used for the approaches to the new bridge. The rest was deposited in spoil areas on the north bank of the canal just outside the village. All equipment and tracks were removed by May 15, 1912, the start of the shipping season.

The expansion of the canal through the village eliminated several structures along the south side of the canal. The Hawkins Block was razed, and the former Chadwick Block was cut up into three sections then moved to other locations. When the canal was constructed through the village, the walls were built vertically to accommodate bridges and docking areas for industry.

North Street, which ran along the south side of the canal from West Avenue near the Main Street bridge to the middle of the photograph, was removed. The triangular building in the middle of the photograph was moved from West Avenue near the Main Street bridge and was later the home of the K.O.D. (Knocks Out Dirt) soap factory. North Street from the factory on was renamed Roselawn Avenue. The factory is a residential building today.

In 1902, a bedstead truss lift bridge was installed over the Erie Canal at Fullam's Basin. During canal reconstruction in 1913, workers dug a new path for the canal in this area just east of the old canal bed (now Perinton Park and surroundings). To span the new trench, a new steel truss bridge was erected on the east side of the older bridge, which was then removed. In 1975, Fairport Road was widened, and the 1913 bridge was replaced.

The bridge known as Baker's or Cobb's bridge was replaced by a steel lattice truss bridge in 1912. By the early 1980s, the bridge became so decrepit that some citizens lobbied the state legislature to replace it. They sent potatoes to legislators, which represented an incident on an old state-owned bridge where a truckload of potatoes fell through the bridge's deck. A new bridge was installed in 1983.

As the canal was deepened, accommodations had to be made for creeks that flowed under the canal. Thomas Creek, just east of the village of Fairport, is one of four creeks in Perinton where culverts were built to carry them under the canal. Large concrete culverts were built, separated by timbers. Today no traces of these culverts can be seen, and there is stagnant water on both sides of the canal near this spot.

At Bushnell's Basin in the southwest corner of Perinton, concrete slabs were constructed early in 1912 in an earthen aqueduct that carried the canal over Irondequoit Creek. By September 12, 1912, leaks developed between the slabs, and water from the canal eroded the soil underneath. So much soil eroded that on September 12, the slabs fell of their own weight and a major break developed, which closed the canal.

After the break, the soil was replaced and then stabilized by pounding large logs into the loose soil. In August 1913, several thousand round logs were delivered to Bushnell's Basin to help stabilize the soil before reconnecting the canal bed.

Because there were only three months left in the shipping season, workers quickly stabilized the earthen banks and built a wooden flume to bridge the gap in the canal. The flume was narrow and allowed only one barge to pass at a time. This structure was removed in 1918, more than five years after the break. Today one can still see the concrete vertical wall that connected with the flume.

This is the site of the canal break. A design was approved in July 1913 to replace the earthen aqueduct with one of concrete. Contract 111 called for seven arches, each 75 feet long, which would carry a concrete trough 96 feet wide by 16½ feet deep across the valley. The contract was never awarded, and the great embankment remains an earthen structure with a concrete trough. The concrete slabs dislodged by the break of 1912 remain buried in the embankment under the new trough.

URBAN RENEWAL

West Side Main St., Fairport, N.Y.

This was about the way the village of Fairport looked for the last half of the 19th century and most of the 20th century. The most impressive and interesting buildings were found on South Main Street in a one-block area from the canal to the bank building. The most prominent merchants and shops were found along this stretch of road.

Starting with the picture on page 77, there is a noticeable evolution of the South Main Street business district in 1900, at its razing in 1977, and in the present day. The multiple buildings were replaced with a single-building shopping mall designed to look like a small canal town. The entrances to shops facing Main Street shown here are below grade and entrances to the shops on the second floor are on the back of the building.

This scene of South Main Street taken from the north shows buildings virtually unchanged for 60 years. The only building to be razed from 1850 to 1910 is the fourth building from the right, which was the former Fullam Block. In the early 1900s, this was Abe Taylor's barbershop. In 1908, Taylor sold his shop, moved to Rochester, and entered New York State politics. This building was torn down to make room for the Clark Block two years later in 1910.

From left to right are the corner of the Bown Block, the Clark Block, the Ives Block, the Smith-Morey Block, and the Seeley Block. In 1920, the Clark Block was the scene of an incident between two young men at a dance that grew into a gang fight several days later. The Ives Block was the home of John Ives, a Fairport silversmith, from 1864 to 1871. Today the Fairport Village Landing Mall has small shops on the lower level, the library, and an urban park on the far right.

URBAN RENEWAL

The Bown Block was an attractive redbrick building constructed in 1890. It is decorated for the 13th annual fireman's convention of 1908. Constructed by businessman George Bown, the building once held the post office, the Grange hall, and grocery and drugstores. Bown also ran a carriage shop in a building in the back. For several years, the Fairport Public Library was located in this building. Today at the Fairport Village Landing Mall, there is a restaurant on the site.

The west side of South Main Street looking north shows the Fairport Laundry, former home of the A&P grocery store. This building replaced the residence of DeWitt Becker and the former Becker Bank.

Tony's Shoe Repair was in the Adams Block next to the Bown Block. Today there is a restaurant and small shops as part of the Fairport Village Landing Mall.

One of the more controversial buildings to be taken down for urban renewal was the Price-Wagner house. This structure from about 1850 was once the home of Dr. George Price and later Judge Robert Wagner. Petitions were signed and efforts made to save the building for a community center or museum. The engineer in charge of designing the new shopping mall said the entire project would be in jeopardy if the building was not removed. All efforts to save the building failed, and it was destroyed in 1977.

The only surviving building from the urban renewal zone is the Fairport National Bank building. This buff brick building with granite trim was constructed in the Italian Renaissance style in 1924. It was designated as a local landmark in the village of Fairport in 2008. Saving bank buildings in urban renewal projects was fairly typical at the time. Another urban renewal project in neighboring East Rochester saw the survival of its bank building, which is now in the middle of a parking lot.

Across South Main Street from the canal, many vintage storefronts were taken down over the years. The last building on the right is now the site of the Fairport Village Hall. The children are racing down the street around 1900 just before the coming of the traditional Fourth of July parade.

From left to right are the canal tower, Quality Cleaners building, Best-Beeton Block, and Storms-Ives Block. Many old-time residents remember the Best-Beeton Block as the home of Rudins Clothing store. Over the years, owners added large signs to attract customers and modernized their storefronts. A typical exterior addition to the store facades was a thin facing stone. The Storms-Ives building sports a bluestone covering in the front. The complex that replaced these buildings is called Packett's Landing.

The Mayfair Department Store on South Main Street included an addition to the front of a former residence. Later the front of the store was remodeled using a covering of gray asphalt siding. The pattern on the siding simulates stone. This area is now the entrance to Packett's Landing and off-street parking.

The Erie Canal stimulated many businesses by bringing in raw materials from the west. This site was the former Dobbin and Moore Lumber Company, which operated on this spot from 1879 to 1904. Lumber was transported from the forests of Michigan and used for building and for the company's sash and door business. In 1940, the yard was known as the Hanby-Dudley Lumber Company. This prime canal property is now a dock area and restaurant.

West Avenue was another bustling business district in the village affected by urban renewal. The South Main Street lift bridge is on the right. A curve built into the metal bridge eased traffic down West Avenue. In 1989, urban renewal shut the street off from South Main Street and created Kennelly Park, which was named after former village mayor Vincent Kennelly who served from 1982 to 1989. The park has a gazebo and overlooks the Erie Canal to the right.

The Chadwick-Schummers Block was one of the earliest sets of business buildings in the village of Fairport. The three distinctive sets of buildings were built in the 1850s. For more than 80 years, there was a hardware store in this block from Schummer's Hardware Store in 1889 to Fairport Hardware in the 1970s. The block was razed in 1975 and replaced with Kennelly Park.

There have been several buildings on the south side of West Avenue at the corner of Perrin Street. This was the first home of Joseph Yale Parce, who later moved to a mansion on North Main Street. In 1946, Dr. Charles Whitney bought the house, razed it, and constructed an office building designed by local architect Henry Martin. In the late 1970s, the site became the back corner of a supermarket, a part of the Fairport Village Landing Mall.

From left to right are Shaw's Hall, the Jacobson Block, and the Laird house. Shaw's Hall began as a one-story building moved here from North Main Street in 1854. Later a former church building moved in 1868 from West Church Street was added. The Jacobson Block was owned by Sam Jacobson, who ran a tailoring business. The Gothic Revival Laird house was the home of William Laird, who ran a carting company. Today this area is the back of the Fairport Village Landing Mall.

The Butler Block at 15–19 West Avenue was owned by Ben Butler, who sold sewing machines and hung wallpaper. In 1866, Will O. Greene published the *Monroe County Mail* here, and from 1910 to 1918, it was the office for the Kerbaugh Company, contractors for the improvement of the Erie Canal. In 1937, the building housed the Steven and Maine Bowling Alley, known later as the Fairport Bowling Alley. The building was destroyed by fire in 1973 and demolished.

This building was originally a shirtwaist factory and was located in the middle of a block behind the buildings of West Avenue and South Main Street. Gundlach Manufacturing Company purchased the building in 1935 and manufactured professional cameras and lenses there. An entrance to the underground garage is on the site today.

The white Greek Revival house, seen across the street, was one of three houses built in a row by James Perrin around 1856. Each house had the exact same floor plan. The house was owned by Dr. Clapp, whose daughter Charlotte lived there all her life. She was the town of Perinton historian for 30 years. The houses were replaced with a low berm and the entrance from Perrin Street to the Fairport Village Landing Mall.

ACROSS AMERICA, PEOPLE ARE DISCOVERING SOMETHING WONDERFUL. *THEIR HERITAGE.*

Arcadia Publishing is the leading local history publisher in the United States. With more than 3,000 titles in print and hundreds of new titles released every year, Arcadia has extensive specialized experience chronicling the history of communities and celebrating America's hidden stories, bringing to life the people, places, and events from the past. To discover the history of other communities across the nation, please visit:

www.arcadiapublishing.com

Customized search tools allow you to find regional history books about the town where you grew up, the cities where your friends and family live, the town where your parents met, or even that retirement spot you've been dreaming about.